Wealth Wrap: Hack Savings, Crush Investments, and Retire Early

Proven Strategies to Accelerate Your Money Goals and Ditch the 9-5 Forever

KULDEVA I

First Edition 2026

This book is also available on Amazon Kindle.

CONTENTS

PREFACE: 01

CHAPTER 1: UNDERSTANDING PERSONAL FINANCE: **03**

CHAPTER 2: BUDGETING BASICS: **05**

CHAPTER 3: SAVING STRATEGIES: **14**

CHAPTER 4: MANAGING DEBT: **19**

CHAPTER 5: INVESTING FUNDAMENTALS: **24**

CHAPTER 6: RETIREMENT PLANNING: **30**

CHAPTER 7: INSURANCE CONSIDERATIONS: **36**

CHAPTER 8: NAVIGATING FINANCIAL CRISES: **42**

CHAPTER 9: BEHAVIOURAL FINANCE: **46**

CHAPTER 10: THE FUTURE OF PERSONAL FINANCE: **49**

Preface

Thank you for picking up this book. I sincerely hope the strategies shared here help you in the same way they have helped me and many others who followed them. My intention is that this book brings a lasting change in your mindset and financial behavior.

In life, there is never a fixed amount of money that can satisfy all our dreams. We are constantly influenced by attractive advertisements, tempting offers, and the urge to try new things. As a result, our needs keep growing or changing, and we often lose focus on financial planning and money management. It begins to feel like we always need more, and that our goals may not be achievable within the time we have.

However, the truth is—you can take control of your finances and your life. This begins with changing the way you manage your money and handle your responsibilities. Real control comes when you consciously limit unnecessary expenses and choose to spend only on things that truly add value to your life.

Over the years, I have learned money management through personal experience. I have read various books and articles, followed expert advice, and then develop my own strategies for different financial goals—whether it is budgeting, retirement planning, or managing day-to-day expenses.

Every idea and strategy mentioned in this book has been personally tested by me. I have adapted them based on my needs and financial situation, and only those approaches that worked effectively have been included here.

You may find some of these concepts familiar. However, the goal of this book is to increase awareness and encourage you to take practical steps towards financial control. When you consistently apply these strategies and turn them into habits, you will notice a significant shift in your financial mindset and discipline.

A brief introduction about myself—I come from an IT background and have significant experience in that field. Alongside my professional journey, I have always had a strong interest in personal finance. Initially, my approach was not structured. I explored stocks, then mutual funds, and gradually learned how to manage income and expenses more effectively. The learnings shared in this book are a result of this continuous journey.

Finally, I would like to say that the key to success is action. The strategies in this book can deliver effective and predictable results—but only when you apply them with consistency and discipline.

Chapter 1: Understanding Personal Finance

Defining Personal Finance

In the journey of life, financial stability plays a very important role. It's like the strong foundation of a house—if it's solid, you can build your dreams, comfort, and peace of mind on top of it without worry. Personal finance isn't just some boring topic about saving a few rupees or investing in stocks. No, it's something that touches every part of our life. From buying chai and samosa every evening to planning for your kid's education or your own retirement, everything connects back to how smartly you handle your money.

At its core, personal finance means understanding how to earn, spend, save, and grow your money wisely. It's about making sure every single rupee you earn has a purpose. Think about it: in India, we often say "paise ki Kimat samjho." It's not just about how much salary you get from your job or business—it's about managing what you already have. For example, if you're earning 50,000 rupees a month but spending 45,000 on unnecessary gadgets, fancy clothes, or eating out at malls, you'll always feel broke. But if you start tracking your expenses, cut down on those impulse buys, and save even 5,000-10,000, you slowly feel in control. That control brings real peace—no more late-night stress over bills.

Imagine personal finance as a guiding compass in life's busy market. Without it, you're just wandering—like taking an auto without knowing the destination. You might earn well, say 1 lakh a month, but end up stuck in debt traps from easy loans or credit cards. I've seen friends buy bikes or phones on EMI, thinking "bahut aasan hai," only to struggle with monthly payments later. But when you learn basic principles—like the 50/30/20 rule (50% for needs like rent and groceries, 30% for wants like movies, 20% for savings)—you get clarity. Suddenly, your decisions support your future: saving for a house down payment or an emergency fund for medical costs, which we all know can hit hard in India.

In today's world, with apps like Paytm, PhonePe, and endless loan ads on Instagram, it's super easy to fall into traps. One swipe, and your money's gone on sales or quick fixes. Personal finance teaches discipline. It helps you spot the difference between what you *want* (like that new iPhone) and what you *truly need* (like a good health insurance policy). This one habit can change your life completely—less debt, more savings, and no living paycheck to paycheck.

Most importantly, personal finance is personal. Your story is different from your neighbor's. Maybe you have aging parents to support, or you're a single earner in a joint family. Your income, responsibilities, and dreams—like funding a wedding or starting a small shop—are unique. So, your plan should be too. Start small: make a monthly budget on a notebook or app, avoid high-interest loans, and invest in simple things like PPF, RD, or mutual funds via SIP

In the end, personal finance isn't just about money—it's about freedom, confidence, and living life on your own terms. When you master it, you don't just manage rupees... you start managing your life better. No more depending on others, more trips to Goa with family, and real Swatantra. Start today, bhai—your future self will thank you.

Chapter 2: Budgeting Basics

Creating a Budget

Tracking Expenses

Adjusting Your Budget

Almost every household tries to prepare a budget, but following it consistently is often the real challenge. There are many methods to build a budget, yet the basics remain the same. Let's walk through a simple, practical way to set up your personal household budget.

Step 1: List your income.

Start by noting all sources of income—for example, your salary (net amount credited to your bank), rental income if any, or your spouse's salary. Since we're focusing on personal finance, children's income (if they earn) isn't considered here. Suppose you and your spouse both earn—add these amounts together to calculate your household income.

Step 2: Prioritize savings

The golden rule is save before you spend. Most people spend first and save what's left, but it works far better the other way around. Aim to save anywhere between 20% to 50% of your total income. You may start small but set 50% as a Mid-term target and try to move closer to it over time.

Step 3: Plan your expenses

The remaining amount is what you'll use for expenses. A simple and effective way to create this is through Excel sheets (though there are many budgeting tools available too). Create different sheets to organize your finances clearly:

1. Savings Sheet – Record the money you set aside every month.
2. Monthly Expenses Sheet – Note down recurring costs like household help salaries, utility bills (mobile, internet, electricity), groceries, fuel, milk, insurance premiums, travel, and other day-to-day expenses. Also have columns with heading of each Month like April - March
3. Annual/Quarterly Expenses Sheet – Capture expenses that occur occasionally, such as vehicle servicing, property tax, advance tax, festival celebrations, birthdays, anniversaries, and vacations.
4. EMI Sheet – List out all your loans (home, car, education, personal) along with their monthly EMI amounts.
5. Insurance Sheet – Record all policies you hold (life, term, health, vehicle, etc.) with their premium amounts. To manage premiums better, add them up for the year and divide by 12. Save this amount every month so that funds are always ready when the premium is due. This prevents last-minute struggles to pay large premiums.
6. Net Worth Sheet – Track your overall financial position by listing your assets (cash, FDs, RDs, mutual funds, stocks, gold, property, crypto, etc.) and your liabilities (loans, borrowed money, guarantees given, etc.). This sheet gives you a clear snapshot of where you stand financially

This structure not only helps you stay disciplined but also ensures you're prepared for regular as well as unexpected expenses—while steadily building wealth.

Below is the Pic will help you with above illustration.

Work sheet –

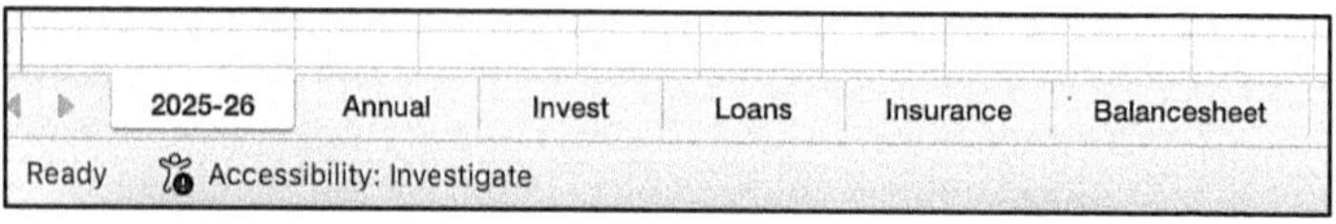

Monthly Budget –

	A	B	C	D	E	F	G	H	I	J	K	L	M	N	O
1	Regular Expense		New Amount	Apr	May	Jun	Jul	Aug	Sep	Oct	Nov	Dec	Jan	Feb	Mar
2															
3	Car Wash														
4	Bai														
5	milk														
6	Mobile Bill														
7	electricity														
8	Pune Gas Bill														
9	Tata sky +Nflix+Hotstar+Lnkdn														
10	Gujarat Belectricity bill														
11	Conv														
12	LKO Tax														
13	Society charge Colori														
14	Medical														
15	Household														
16	Mom														
17	Insurance														
18	RS														
19	Misc														
20	TOTAL														
21															

Annual budget –

	A	B	C	D	E	F	G	H	I	J	K	L	M	N	O
1	Annual Expense		AMOUNT	Apr	May	Jun	Jul	Aug	Sep	Oct	Nov	Dec	Jan	Feb	Mar
2															
3	Car Service														
4	Diwali/Holi														
5	Birthday														
6	Anniversary														
7	Travel														
8	House Tax														
9	Misc/Gift														
10															
11	Savings														
12															

Investment -

	A	B	C	D	E	F	G	H	I	J	K	L	M	N
70	Months of 2025-26	Amount	Apr	May	Jun	Jul	Aug	Sep	Oct	Nov	Dec	Jan	Feb	Mar
81														
82	Reccuring Deposit													
83	Fixed Deposit													
84	Mutual Fund SIP													
85	Stocks													
86	Gold													
87	Misc.													
88														

Loans –

	A	B	D	E	F	G	H	I	J	K	L	M	N	O	P
74	Months of 2023-24		Amount	Apr	May	Jun	Jul	Aug	Sep	Oct	Nov	Dec	Jan	Feb	Mar
75	Loans														
76	Home Loan														
77	Perossnal Loan														
78	Commercial Loan														
79	Car Loan														
80	Two Wehcler Loan														
81	Other loans														
82	Total														
83															

Balance Sheet –

	A	B	C	D	E	F	G	H
1			ASSET				DEBT	
2								
3		Shares				HL IDK 1		
4		MF				Office Space		
5		savings(cash)				HL IDK 2		
6		Insurance						
7		AK PPF						
8		Jwellery						
9		EPF				Mosi		
10		SGB				Taruna Di		
11		FD				Rishu		
12		Property 1						
13		NCD						
14		Property 2 Land						
15						G Total		
16		Total						
17								
18		Property3- Self Occupied						
19								
20		G Total				liquidable	0	
21								
22								
23								
24						Networth	0	
25								

Insurance –

Name	Insurance Tyoe	Insurance Amount	Policy Number	Prmium	Due Date	Payment term
Yourself	Term Plan	XXXX				Yearly
Wife Name	Term Plan	XXXX				Yearly
Kids Name	Education plan	XXXX				Monthly
Wife Name	Car Insurance	XXXX				Yearly
Youself	Two weheler	XXXX				Half yearly

The next and most crucial step is **not just creating a budget but sticking to it consistently and tracking your expenses with discipline**. A budget on paper has no meaning unless it is followed in practice.

In most households, the majority of expenses occur in the first 10 days of the month—expenses like bill payments, groceries, EMIs, and household salaries. This makes it the perfect window to update your budget sheets. Between the 1st and the 10th of every month, revisit each sheet—Savings, Monthly Expenses, Annual Expenses, EMIs, and Insurance. The only exception is your Net Worth sheet, which doesn't need frequent changes and should ideally be reviewed once every quarter.

When you update, record the **actual expenses** under each head in the respective month's column. For example, if your electricity bill was budgeted at ₹2,500 but came to ₹2,900, enter the actual figure. Doing this regularly helps you see patterns in your spending and immediately highlights where fluctuations are happening.

Now, if a particular expense keeps varying for three months or more, it's a signal to dig deeper. Maybe your fuel costs have gone up because of longer commutes, or your grocery bills have risen due to price hikes or lifestyle changes. Once you identify the cause, adjust the budgeted amount to reflect reality. This makes your budget more practical and keeps it aligned with your actual lifestyle.

By the end of the month, you can clearly see how much you planned to spend and how much you actually spent.

However, one rule is non-negotiable: **never reduce your savings by more than 1%** to cover extra expenses. Savings are your financial backbone—whether for emergencies, investments, or future goals. If you need to rebalance your budget, cut back on discretionary spending (like dining out, entertainment, or non-essential shopping), but protect your savings.

By consistently following this system—updating monthly, adjusting when needed, and guarding your savings—you'll not only gain control over your money but also build long-term financial stability with confidence.

Below is real example of the tracking and adjusting the budget.

Imagine a family with two income earners—let's say their combined monthly income is ₹1,20,000. They've set a target to save 30% (₹36,000) right at the start of the month and use the rest for expenses.

Month 1 (January)

- **Grocery budget:** ₹10,000 → **Actual:** ₹11,200 (slightly overshot due to festive season shopping)
- **Fuel budget:** ₹5,000 → **Actual:** ₹4,800 (within range)
- **Electricity bill budget:** ₹2,500 → **Actual:** ₹3,100 (higher than expected due to heater usage in winter)

They update these figures in their Excel sheets between the 1st and 10th. No changes yet—just observation.

Month 2 (February)

- **Grocery budget:** ₹10,000 → **Actual:** ₹11,000 (again slightly above)
- **Fuel budget:** ₹5,000 → **Actual:** ₹5,600 (increased travel to attend family functions)
- **Electricity bill budget:** ₹2,500 → **Actual:** ₹2,900

Now two categories (groceries + fuel) have crossed their budgeted amounts for a second month. Still not alarming, but worth keeping an eye on.

Month 3 (March)

- **Grocery budget:** ₹10,000 → **Actual:** ₹11,300
- **Fuel budget:** ₹5,000 → **Actual:** ₹5,700
- **Electricity bill budget:** ₹2,500 → **Actual:** ₹2,400

At this point, groceries and fuel have overshot **three months in a row**. Clearly, the original budget no longer reflects reality.

Why Tracking is important?

- **Gives clear visibility**- Most people only have a rough idea of where their money goes. Tracking shows the reality. You see exactly how much you spend on food delivery, shopping, or impulsive online buys.
- **Helps control overspending**- When you see your numbers in front of you, you naturally become more careful. You think twice before ordering again or buying something you don't really need.
- **Makes your budget realistic-** Many budgets fail because they are just guesses. Actual tracking shows your real patterns, so you can set practical limits for groceries, travel, entertainment, etc., that match your lifestyle.

- **Supports your financial goals-** If you want to save for an emergency fund, a trip, a car, or a house, tracking helps you find money to redirect from wasteful areas towards these goals every month.
- **Reduces stress and surprises-** When you know your fixed costs and your usual spending, month-end does not feel so scary. You can plan for upcoming fees, repairs, gifts, and avoid last-minute panic or borrowing.
- **Builds discipline and habits-** Writing down expenses daily or weekly makes you more mindful. Over time, you automatically start choosing better options—like cooking at home more, cancelling unused subscriptions, or avoiding high-interest debt.

·**Adjustment Steps**

- Increase **grocery budget** to ₹11,500 (instead of ₹10,000).
- Increase **fuel budget** to ₹6,000 (instead of ₹5,000).
- Keep electricity at ₹2,500 since fluctuations are seasonal.

But instead of reducing savings, look at their **entertainment budget** (₹8,000) and trim it down to ₹6,500 to balance the increase.

· **Results**

- Savings remain at ₹36,000 every month.
- The budget now matches actual lifestyle needs, reducing stress.
- At the end of the quarter, they also review the **Net Worth Sheet** to check progress on assets vs liabilities.

Benefits of doing adjustments in budgets

- **You align with real life-** When your income, prices, or responsibilities change, an updated budget matches your current situation instead of an old, unrealistic plan.

- **You free up money for goals**- Cutting or reducing unnecessary expenses lets you move that money to savings, investments, or debt repayment, helping you reach goals faster.

- **You reduce stress and uncertainty-** A budget that actually works (because it's updated) gives more peace of mind, since you know bills, EMIs, and priorities are covered and surprises are less likely.

- **You improve money habits over time-** Regular reviewing and adjusting trains you to be more intentional with spending, improves decision-making, and slowly builds stronger financial discipline.

Chapter 3: Saving Strategies

The Importance of Saving

Building an Emergency Fund

Long-term Saving Goals

Automating Savings

Savings have always been seen as a foundation of financial stability. Traditionally, families depend on gold, land, or fixed deposits as their main ways for wealth creation. The culture of setting aside a portion of income, even in modest households, is rooted because financial security has often been viewed as protection not just for an individual, but for the entire family. Unlike in some countries where credit plays a bigger role, Indians have historically leaned on savings before taking on debt.

Savings also play a critical role in meeting life's milestones. From children's education and marriages to buying a home or supporting aging parents, every big life event often rely on years of disciplined saving. For many, savings represent dignity and independence, ensuring that family responsibilities can be fulfilled without financial strain. In a society where unexpected medical expenses or job losses can put pressure on households, having reserves acts as an essential buffer.

Recently, the approach to saving in India has evolved. While earlier generations preferred safe, low-risk instruments like post office schemes, provident funds, and bank deposits, today's younger population is increasingly exploring mutual funds, SIPs, and even equity investments. Yet, the core principle remains the same: savings are the starting point for wealth creation and financial security. By balancing traditional safety with modern investment opportunities, Indian households are earning to make their savings work harder while still holding on to the age-old wisdom of living within one's means.

From traditional times to the present day, savings have always played a crucial role in helping individuals and families navigate difficult or uncertain situations. What we now call an *emergency fund* is essentially the same concept—money kept aside to protect us during tough times. Traditionally, all savings acted as this cushion, but today the idea is more structured and intentional.

The general rule suggests keeping 3–6 months of your income in an emergency fund. However, with changing lifestyles and aspirations—such as exploring new career opportunities, starting something on your own, or aiming for early retirement it makes sense to aim for more. For some, this could even mean setting aside 2–3 years of income.

Why an emergency fund is important?

- Acts like a safety net Life is unpredictable- sudden job loss, medical emergency, urgent travel, or big repair can come anytime, and an emergency fund helps you handle these without panic.
- Protects your long-term goals- Without this fund, you may be forced to break your investments meant for goals like

education, house, or retirement, which disturbs your entire financial planning.

- Helps you avoid debt- In emergencies many people swipe credit cards or take personal loans at high interest; an emergency fund lets you pay from your own pocket and avoid the debt trap.
- Gives peace of mind-Just knowing you have some months of expenses kept aside reduces stress and fear about "what if something goes wrong," and helps you take calmer decisions.
- Supports you during income loss- If your salary stops, business slows, or you cannot work for some time, this fund helps you manage basic expenses like rent, food, and utilities till things become normal

To build such a fund, you can start with a systematic investment plan (SIP) in a reliable mutual fund. The idea is not to chase high returns but to create the corpus quickly. Once you've reached your target, shift the amount to highly liquid instruments like fixed deposits (FDs) or liquid funds. Another option is to begin with a recurring deposit and later move it into an FD. A good approach is to allocate 25–30% of your savings initially toward this goal, and once you've built your fund, reduce the contribution to around 5%.

Liquidity is key.

Your emergency fund should always be easily accessible. One practical way to divide it is: 25% in a savings account for immediate needs, 25% in FDs for safety, and 50% in a good liquid fund. Of course, this allocation can be adjusted depending on individual preference. Most importantly, the fund should be touched only in genuine emergencies such as job loss, pursuing new opportunities, or medical situations not fully covered by insurance. By steadily growing it 5–10% every year, you ensure that your emergency fund remains relevant and strong enough to safeguard your future.

Long-term saving goals are the big financial targets we set for our future—things that usually take five years or more to achieve. These could be buying a home, funding your child's education, planning for retirement, or even starting your own business someday. Unlike short-term savings, which cover emergencies or monthly needs, long-term goals are about creating stability and security for the years ahead.

The real value of long-term savings lies in the way small, regular contributions can grow over time. Thanks to compounding, even small amounts saved consistently can turn into a large sum. This not only helps in reaching life milestones but also reduces the need to depend on loans or debt. Knowing that your future plans are steadily being funded also brings a sense of peace and confidence.

In India, long-term savings become even more important because we often don't have the kind of social security benefits that some other countries provide. Rising costs of healthcare, higher education, and family responsibilities mean that savings play a big role in maintaining financial independence. By starting early and sticking to your plan, you can secure your family's needs and enjoy more freedom in the later years of life.

Long-term saving amount should always be 35% -40% of your savings and should be invested in high return and steady growth providing instruments like Good Mutual funds or a Equity linked saving schemes, Provident Fund, Personal Provident Fund, Gold or real estate and may be more of them. It all depends on what kind of a person you are and in what age group you are saving like senior people are more conservative and prefer to invest in EPF and PPF more as compared to MF.

Automating your savings is one of the easiest ways to build wealth because it takes away the need to think about it every month. Instead of saving whatever money is left after spending, you save first. As soon as your salary comes in, a fixed amount is automatically moved to your savings or investment account.

The biggest benefit of this is consistency. Many people plan to save but end up spending more than expected or simply forget. When your savings are automatic, you don't have to rely on memory or discipline—it just happens. Even small amounts saved regularly can grow into a large sum over time.

It also makes life simpler. You don't have to keep deciding every month whether you should save or not. That decision is already taken care of. This reduces stress and helps you stay on track without much effort.

Another advantage is that it helps control unnecessary spending. When money is moved out of your main account quickly, you're less likely to spend it on things you don't really need. You naturally adjust your spending based on what's left.

In the long run, this habit can help you achieve important financial goals like building an emergency fund, saving for retirement, or planning big purchases. Automating your savings makes the whole process easy, steady, and stress-free.

There are several practical ways to do this like SIP, Recurring Deposit, Auto transfer to Fixed Deposit and other instruments.

If you are investing in Stocks, then SEP is also an option for automating your investment in stocks.

You can create Fixed Deposit of may be 10 million INR and then interest earn put of it can be move into Mutual Funds in SIP Format. This will help you keep principal amount with you interest to move away to earn more returns.

Chapter 4: Managing Debt

Understanding Different Types of Debt

Strategies for Paying Off Debt

Avoiding Future Debt

Debt is not always a bad word. It comes in different forms, each with its own rules, costs, and risks. The key lies in how you use it. Think of debt like fire: if used carefully, it can cook your food and keep you warm; if left unattended, it can burn everything you have.

Good Debt vs. Bad Debt

Broadly, debt can be split into two categories: good debt and bad debt.

- **Good Debt**
  Good debt is an investment in your future. It helps you create value, either by building an asset or increasing your earning potential.
  - **Examples:**
    - Education loans that open doors to better career opportunities.
    - Home loans that allow you to own property, which often appreciates in value over time.

        - Business loans that support growth and expansion.

The hallmark of good debt is that it pays you back in some way—either financially or by improving your quality of life.

- **Bad Debt**
  Bad debt, on the other hand, drains your finances without leaving anything valuable behind. It usually funds short-term desires rather than long-term gains.
    - **Examples:**
        - High-interest credit card debt from lifestyle spending.
        - Personal loans for weddings, vacations, or luxury items.
        - Payday or instant loans with extreme interest rates.

The problem with bad debt is that it leaves you paying more tomorrow for something that has already lost value today.

Secured vs. Unsecured Debt

Another way to look at debt is whether it is secured or unsecured.

- **Secured Debt** is backed by collateral. For instance, a home loan is secured by the property itself, and a car loan by the vehicle. Because the lender has something to fall back on, interest rates are usually lower.

- **Unsecured Debt** requires no collateral, which makes it riskier for lenders and more expensive for borrowers. Credit cards, personal loans, and loans for lifestyle expenses fall into this category.

Smart Strategies for Repaying Debt

Once you've taken on debt, the real challenge is paying it off efficiently. Here are some proven approaches:

1. **Debt Snowball Method**
   Focus on clearing the smallest loan first while paying minimums on others. Once it's gone, roll that payment into the next-smallest loan. The quick wins give you motivation and momentum.

2. **Debt Avalanche Method**
   Pay off the loan with the highest interest rate first. This saves the most money in the long run because it attacks the most expensive debt first.

3. **Consolidation or Balance Transfer**
   If you have multiple high-interest debts, consider combining them into a single lower-interest loan. Some credit cards also allow balance transfers at lower rates for a limited time.

4. **Step-Up Repayments**
   Each time you close a loan, redirect that EMI into the next loan. Over time, your repayment power snowballs and you clear debts much faster.

5. **Invest Alongside Repayment**
   Instead of increasing your EMI every time, consider investing the freed-up amount in a SIP or recurring deposit. When the corpus grows, you can make a lump-sum payment toward your principal, directly reducing your interest burden.

Practical Habits to Stay Debt-Free

- Keep EMIs within 30–40% of your monthly income. Anymore, and repayment may become stressful.
- Always maintain an emergency fund. This ensures you don't fall back on credit cards or personal loans when unexpected expenses come up.
- Avoid borrowing for depreciating assets. Gadgets, furniture, or luxury spending lose value quickly, but the loan lingers.
- Automate payments. Set up auto-debits to avoid missed EMIs and late fees.
- Celebrate milestones. Closing even one small loan is a big step forward—acknowledge it.

Final Thought

Managing debt is not about avoiding it completely, but about handling it wisely. Debt can be useful when used for the right reasons, like education, a home, or growing a business. The problem starts when debt becomes uncontrolled and begins to affect your peace of mind and financial stability.

The key is to stay aware of how much you owe and have a clear plan to repay it. Always try to pay your dues on time and avoid relying too much on credit cards or loans for everyday expenses. Small habits, like tracking your spending and sticking to a budget, can make a big difference over time.

It's also important to prioritize high-interest debts first, as they grow faster and can become a burden quickly. At the same time, try to build a small emergency fund so that unexpected expenses don't push you deeper into debt.

Most importantly, be patient and consistent. Getting out of debt is a journey, not a one-time action. With discipline, smart decisions, and a focused approach, you can gradually reduce your debt and move towards a more secure and stress-free financial future.

Debt is a tool. The outcome depends entirely on how you use it. Borrow to build your future, not to finance fleeting pleasures. Pair every loan with a repayment plan, and whenever possible, with a parallel investment. That way, you'll not only free yourself from debt faster but also create a foundation of financial strength for the years ahead.

Chapter 5: Investing Fundamentals

Why Invest?

Types of Investments

Risk vs. Reward

Creating an Investment Plan

Investment is one of the most significant pillars of financial growth and stability. While it has become a buzzword in the world of finance, its importance goes far beyond trend or jargon. At its core, investing is about making your money work for you and ensuring long-term financial well-being.

Why should one invest?

- **To Beat Inflation**

Over time, the value of money erodes due to inflation. Simply saving is not enough, as your purchasing power decreases year after year. Investing allows your money to grow at a rate higher than inflation, protecting and enhancing its value.

- **To Create Wealth**

  Investments unlock the power of compounding, helping your savings multiply over time. This is the key to building wealth and generating more money from the money you already own.

- **To Achieve Financial Goals**

  Whether it's buying a house, purchasing a car, planning for retirement, or fulfilling personal aspirations, investments help you reach your short-term and long-term goals systematically.

- **For Emergency Preparedness**

  Life is unpredictable. Investments ensure you are financially equipped to handle emergencies such as medical expenses or unexpected job loss, without derailing your future.

- **For Financial Independence**

  The aim of investing is freedom—reaching a point where your money earns for you. Financial independence means you can retire on your own terms and live without worrying about day-to-day expenses.

Now that we understand **why** we should invest, the next step is to know **where** to invest. For that, it's important to understand the different types of investments available. Broadly, investments can be categorized into three types based on the level of risk and return they carry:

1. Low-Risk Investments

These are ideal for individuals who prefer safety and stability over high returns. The risk is minimal, but so are the returns. Such investments are more about preserving capital than multiplying it.

Best for: Risk-averse investors or those saving for short-term needs.

Examples: Savings Bank Accounts, Recurring Deposits (RDs), Fixed Deposits (FDs), and Public Provident Fund (PPF).

2. Medium-Risk Investments

This category suits people looking for a balance between risk and reward. These investments typically provide steady returns over the long term, making them effective tools to beat inflation.

Best for: Investors with a medium risk appetite and long-term financial goals like retirement planning or wealth creation.

Examples: Mutual Funds (debt, hybrid, or index funds), Corporate Bonds, and the National Pension Scheme (NPS).

3. High-Risk Investments

Designed for those with a higher risk appetite, these investments carry the potential for high returns but also greater volatility. They require patience and a long-term perspective to ride out market ups and downs.

Best for: Investors who can tolerate short-term fluctuations in exchange for potentially significant long-term growth.

Examples: Direct Stocks, Equity Mutual Funds, Real Estate, and Cryptocurrencies.

Understanding Risk vs Reward in Investing

When you invest, you're essentially making a choice between **safety** and **growth**. Every investment lies somewhere on the **risk–reward spectrum**.

1. Risk – The Possibility of Loss

Risk is not just about "losing money." It can take different forms:

- **Market Risk** – Prices of stocks or bonds may fall.
- **Credit Risk** – A company or government may fail to pay back loans/bonds.
- **Inflation Risk** – Your returns may be lower than rising prices, reducing purchasing power.
- **Liquidity Risk** – You may not be able to sell your investment quickly when you need cash.

2. Reward – The Potential Gain

Reward is the **return** you expect in exchange for taking risk. This can come in the form of:

- **Interest income** (like in FDs or bonds).
- **Dividends** (from stocks).

- **Capital appreciation** (the value of your investment increasing).
- **Rental income or property appreciation** (in real estate).

3. **The Risk–Reward Trade-Off**

The principle is simple:

- **Low risk = Low but steady returns** (good for safety and short-term goals).
- **Medium risk = Moderate returns** (good for long-term growth with stability).
- **High risk = Potentially high returns** (good for wealth creation, but only if you can handle volatility).

Example:

- If you invest ₹1,00,000 in a **Fixed Deposit**, you might get ₹1,06,000 after a year (safe, predictable).
- If you invest the same in **Mutual Funds**, you might get anywhere between ₹1,08,000 and ₹1,12,000, but it may also drop below ₹1,00,000 in the short term.
- If you put it in Stocks or Crypto, you could end up with ₹1,20,000… or even ₹80,000.

Matching Risk to Your Profile

Not everyone should take the same risk. It depends on:

- Age – Younger people can take more risks (more time to recover losses).
- Financial goals – For short-term needs (like a vacation), low risk is better; for retirement (20+ years away), high risk may be suitable.
- Risk appetite – Some people sleep peacefully only with safe investments others enjoy the thrill of higher risks.
- The Smart Way: Balance
- No smart investor puts all money in one type of risk. A good portfolio balances risk and reward by diversifying:
- Keep some money in low-risk options (safety net).
- Some in medium-risk investments (steady growth).
- Some in high-risk investments (wealth creation).

This way, you protect yourself while also giving your money a chance to grow meaningfully.

Investment planning is important because it turns your **income into wealth**, protects you from inflation, prepares you for emergencies, and helps you achieve financial freedom.

Chapter 6: Retirement Planning

Understanding Retirement Needs

Maximizing Employer Benefits

Adjusting Your Plan Over Time

Retirement is one of the most significant turning points in an individual's life. It marks the transition from decades of routine—waking up early, preparing for office, engaging in endless meetings, sharing laughter and conversations with colleagues, handling professional responsibilities, and receiving a salary at the end of every month—to a phase where life suddenly becomes quieter and slower. This shift can feel liberating for some and unsettling for others, but one truth remains constant: a fulfilling and stress-free retired life doesn't happen by accident. It requires years of thoughtful preparation.

Ideally, by the time a person retires, most major responsibilities should already be completed. This includes paying off home loans and other EMIs, owning a house to live comfortably, ensuring the education of children is completed, and often, seeing them married and settled. In the Indian sub-continent, however, this may not always be the case. Many individuals still have pending obligations even at the time of retirement. If that is so, then it becomes even more important to plan ahead and make sure that those responsibilities can still be met without compromising one's own retired life.

If someone wants to maintain the same standard of living after retirement as they enjoyed during their working years, the preparation must begin as early as possible—ideally from the very first year of employment. The later one starts, the higher the required savings and investment amounts become because the power of compounding has less time to work. Therefore, starting early is the simplest and most effective way to reduce financial pressure in the long run.

Understanding Your Needs at Retirement

- To plan effectively, one must clearly understand the expenses and lifestyle needs during the post-retirement years. These typically fall into a few major categories:

- **Monthly Household Expenses**

These include daily necessities such as groceries, utilities, transportation, and other routine costs required to run the household. Financial planners often estimate that individuals will need about **70%–80% of their current monthly expenses** during retirement. This is because some work-related expenses reduce, but general living costs remain.

- **Medical and Health-Related Costs**

Healthcare becomes one of the biggest expenses after retirement. With increasing age, medical check-ups, treatments, and medications become more frequent. Health insurance premiums also rise significantly, and employer-provided coverage generally stops after superannuation—although some organizations may extend limited coverage for the employee and spouse. Considering the unpredictable nature of health issues, having a strong medical corpus is non-negotiable.

- **Travel, Social Activities, and Hobbies**

Retirement brings more free time, allowing individuals to pursue hobbies, visit relatives, attend family functions, and travel. Whether it's domestic tourism, religious journeys, or exploring international destinations, all such activities incur expenses. Travel costs—such as flights, trains, hotels, local transport, and food—are rising every year, making it important to allocate for this intentionally.

- **Emergency Fund**

An emergency fund acts as a safety buffer during unexpected situations. This could be a medical emergency, a sudden home repair, or any urgent need that demands immediate funds. A well-maintained emergency fund ensures financial stability even during difficult moments.

- **Calculating Your Retirement Corpus**

To live comfortably after retiring, it is essential to calculate the **retirement corpus**, which is the total amount of money you need to accumulate before retiring. The corpus must account for:

- **Inflation**

Inflation steadily increases the cost of living every year. What costs ₹50,000 per month today may cost ₹1.5 lakh or more after 20–25 years. Ignoring inflation is one of the biggest mistakes in retirement planning.

- **Age of Retirement**

Most people retire around 58 or 60, depending on their organization. Some may choose early retirement, whereas others might continue working as consultants or advisors if health permits.

- **Life Expectancy**

This refers to the number of years you expect to live after retirement. For example, if you retire at 60 and expect to live until 85, you must plan for at least **25 years** of expenses—not just survival, but a comfortable life.

By combining these factors, you can determine the required corpus to sustain the same lifestyle even after your salary stops.

Maximizing Employer and Government Benefits

While multiple investment avenues exist, it is wise to first maximize the benefits offered by your employer and the government. These tools are designed to encourage disciplined saving.

- **EPF and VPF**

The Employee Provident Fund (EPF) is one of the safest and most reliable retirement savings options. Employers contribute 12% of the employee's basic salary, and employees contribute an equal amount. If possible, increasing your contribution through the **Voluntary Provident Fund (VPF)** is highly beneficial, as it earns the same interest as EPF and remains largely tax-free (subject to certain thresholds). It offers assured returns and long-term wealth creation.

- **NPS (National Pension System)**

  NPS is one of the most tax-efficient investment schemes. Employer contributions of up to 10% of basic salary under **Section 80CCD(2)** are tax-free and extremely beneficial.

  Starting NPS early allows more time for compounding. Selecting an **Active Choice** with 50–75% equity allocation (based on age and risk capacity) can offer higher long-term returns.

Tax Advantages

Make full use of tax-saving opportunities:

- **Section 80C** (₹1.5 lakh): Includes EPF, VPF, PPF, life insurance, etc.
- **Section 80CCD(1B)** (additional ₹50,000): Exclusively for NPS.
- **Section 80CCD(2)**: Employer NPS contribution (most tax-efficient benefit).
- These deductions reduce taxable income while simultaneously building your retirement corpus.

Smart Use of Equity Investments

- If investing in equities—either direct stocks or mutual funds—allocate wisely between yourself and your spouse.
  For example, long-term capital gains (LTCG) up to **₹1 lakh per person** per financial year are tax-free. By dividing investments strategically, you can gain a combined tax-free benefit of **₹2 lakh** every year.

- Even after retirement, managing equity exposure smartly ensures capital protection and tax efficiency.

Regular Review and Portfolio Adjustment

- Retirement planning is not a one-time exercise. Investments must be reviewed regularly—ideally once or twice a year to assess returns, adjust risk, and ensure that financial goals remain on track.
- When younger, higher exposure to equities can accelerate wealth creation.
- As retirement approaches, it becomes essential to shift funds gradually toward debt and safer instruments to protect capital and accumulated gains.
- This balanced approach ensures that your retirement corpus remains secure while still growing.

Final Thoughts

Retirement should be a phase of peace, dignity, and comfort—not stress or financial uncertainty. By planning early, calculating needs realistically, and maximizing employer and government benefits, individuals can ensure a financially secure and fulfilling retired life. The key lies in starting early, staying disciplined, and reviewing your plan periodically to stay aligned with changing needs and market conditions.

Chapter 7: Insurance Considerations

Types of Insurance

Evaluating Insurance Needs

Making Claims

Insurance is a financial arrangement that helps protect individuals and businesses from unexpected losses or risks. In insurance, a person pays a fixed amount called a premium to an insurance company. In return, the insurer agrees to compensate for financial losses arising from specific events such as illness, accidents, death, theft, or natural disasters.

Insurance provides financial security, peace of mind, and stability, helping people manage uncertainties in life and plan confidently for the future without sudden economic stress.

Main Types of Insurance

Life Insurance

Provides financial security to your family or helps with long-term savings.

Common Types:

- **Term Insurance** – Pure protection, high cover at low cost
- **Endowment Plans** – Insurance + savings
- **ULIP (Unit Linked Insurance Plan)** – Insurance + market-linked investment
- **Money Back Policy** – Periodic payouts
- **Whole Life Policy** – Coverage up to 99–100 years
- **Pension / Annuity Plans** – Retirement income

Health Insurance

Covers medical expenses due to illness or accidents.

Types:

- Individual Health Insurance
- Family Floater Plan
- Senior Citizen Health Insurance
- Critical Illness Cover
- Top-up & Super Top-up Plans
- Group Health Insurance (Employer provided

Covers:

- Hospitalization
- Pre & post-hospital expenses
- Daycare procedures
- Ambulance charges

General Insurance

Covers non-life risks.

1. **Motor Insurance (Mandatory)**
    - Third-party insurance (legally compulsory)
    - Comprehensive motor insurance

2. **Home Insurance**
    - Building insurance
    - Contents insurance
    - Theft, fire, natural disasters

3. **Travel Insurance**
    - Medical emergencies abroad
    - Trip cancellation
    - Lost baggage, passport

4. **Personal Accident Insurance**
    - Accidental death or disability cover

To promote the importance of insurance and encourage more people to opt for coverage—especially term insurance and health insurance—the Government of India provides several benefits on the premiums paid. Term insurance ensures financial security for dependents, while health insurance helps manage rising healthcare costs. Additionally, insurance premiums qualify for tax benefits under various sections of the Income Tax Act, making insurance not only a protection tool but also a smart financial planning decision.

Tax Benefits on Insurance

Under Income Tax Act:

- **Section 80C** – Life insurance premium (up to ₹1.5 lakh)
- **Section 80D** – Health insurance premium
    - ₹25,000 (self/family)
    - ₹50,000 (senior citizens)
- **Section 10(10D)** – Tax-free maturity/death benefits (conditions apply)

Evaluating Insurance needs

Insurance needs can be evaluated by assessing your income, dependents, existing liabilities, health condition, lifestyle, and future goals. Consider potential risks such as medical emergencies, loss of income, or asset damage, and choose coverage that provides adequate financial protection without overburdening your budget.

How to Choose the Right Insurance

Life Insurance

- Prefer **Term Insurance** for pure protection
- Cover = **10–12× annual income**
- Choose insurer with high **claim settlement ratio**

Health Insurance

- Minimum **₹15–20 lakh cover.**
- **You can opt for top-up insurance which is more cost effective.**
- Check waiting periods & network hospitals
- Prefer policies with **no room rent limits**

Claim Process

The insurance claim process is the procedure through which a policyholder requests financial compensation from the insurer for a covered loss or event. In case of an incident such as hospitalization, accident, or death, the policyholder or nominee must inform the insurance company as soon as possible. Required documents, such as claim forms, medical reports, bills, or death certificates, must be submitted. Claims can be settled either through a cashless facility (for network hospitals) or reimbursement. After verification and assessment, the insurer processes and settles the claim as per policy terms.

Here is a **short and clear sentence**:

Inform the insurer – Notify the insurance company through their app, website, helpline, or agent.

Submit documents – Provide the required forms, bills, and reports.

Choose claim type – Use **cashless treatment** at a network hospital or pay first and claim **reimbursement** later.

Claim settlement – The insurer verifies the details and pays the approved amount as per the policy.

Chapter 8: Navigating Financial Crises

Preparing for Financial Emergencies

Managing During a Crisis

Rebuilding After a Setback

Learning from Crises

Financial emergencies are situations that come without warning and can quickly drain a large part of your savings or investments. Because they can happen to anyone at any time, it is very important to be prepared for them. These emergencies often include loss of a job or a break in regular income, medical problems for yourself or your family, accidents or the sudden death of the main earning member, urgent education expenses, damage to assets such as a house due to fire or theft, and unexpected legal issues. Many of these situations can be handled partly or fully with the help of insurance, which provides financial relief during tough times. However, since insurance may not cover everything, individuals should also maintain personal savings to manage the remaining expenses and stay financially secure.

During a financial crisis or any emergency, having an emergency fund and insurance in place is extremely helpful. However, preparation alone is not enough. It is equally important for an individual to understand how to manage money wisely and make the best use of available financial resources during such times. Proper financial management helps reduce stress, avoid panic decisions, and ensures that essential needs are met without exhausting savings too quickly. By planning expenses carefully, prioritizing critical payments, using savings sensibly, and seeking support where needed, one can navigate a financial emergency more effectively. Below are some practical ways to manage your finances during a crisis and maintain financial stability until the situation improves.

Use of emergency funds- Use your emergency fund only for essential expenses like medical bills and basic needs. If you don't have one, focus on keeping enough cash available and avoid locking money into long-term investments during the crisis.

Controlling Expenses - During a financial crisis, reduce or stop spending on non-essential things like dining out, subscriptions, and luxury items. Concentrate your money on basic needs such as food, rent, electricity, water, and medicines to manage your finances more effectively.

Avoid Panic Decision - Avoid selling your long-term investments out of fear unless it's necessary. Think carefully and review all your options before deciding to withdraw money from fixed deposits or mutual funds, as doing so hastily can hurt your financial stability.

Above all, if possible, try to generate some temporary or short-term source of income. Like consulting, freelancing etc.

Use of Insurance and support system - Make sure to use your health, life, or property insurance whenever it can help. You can also look for support from your employer, family, or any government assistance programs that are available to ease the financial burden.

Getting your finances back on track after a crisis is all about recovering from the setback, planning carefully, and preparing yourself for the future so that you are more secure and less stressed. It means taking a clear look at your current financial situation and making a step-by-step plan to rebuild your savings, pay off debts, and strengthen your financial safety net. With the right approach, you can not only recover from the crisis but also become better prepared to handle any unexpected financial challenges that may come your way in the future.

Start by clearly reviewing your finances. Check how much savings you have left, your income, ongoing expenses, and any debts. Knowing where you stand helps you make realistic decisions.

Create a simple monthly budget based on your current income. Cut down unnecessary expenses and focus on essential spending until your finances improve.

If you have loans or credit card dues, try to pay off high-interest debts first. Speak to banks or lenders if needed to adjust EMIs so repayments remain manageable.

Check your health, life, and asset insurance policies to ensure they provide enough protection. Proper insurance can prevent major financial stress during future emergencies.

Once your income becomes stable, begin saving small amounts regularly. Focus on rebuilding your emergency fund so you have money set aside for unexpected situations in the future.

Once you feel financially stable, slowly resume investing. Start with safer options and then move towards long-term investments for growth. we can become more careful with money and better prepared to face future financial problems with confidence.

Learning from financial crises means looking back at difficult financial times and understanding what went wrong and what could have been done better. Such experiences teach us the importance of saving for emergencies, having proper insurance, and spending money wisely.

Chapter 9: Behavioral Finance

Understanding Financial Behaviors

Overcoming Biases

Building Healthy Financial Habits

Behavioral finance is understanding of how people behave when they make money decisions. It explains how emotions, habits, and personal thinking—such as fear, greed, overconfidence, or panic—affect the way people save, spend, invest, and manage money. Instead of assuming that everyone always makes logical and well-planned financial choices, behavioral finance recognizes that people often act emotionally or impulsively. It helps us understand why investors sometimes make mistakes, follow the crowd, or avoid taking losses, and how these behaviors can influence financial markets and personal financial outcomes. You tend spend more just because of your behavior.

Now that we understand how strongly our emotions influence our financial decisions and spending habits, it becomes important to recognize our personal biases and learn how to overcome them. This helps us clearly see where we may be spending unnecessarily or going beyond our budget or financial capacity. Below are some simple and practical steps to help avoid or manage these biases:

First, before making any financial decision, take a moment to understand what is driving it. Ask yourself whether the decision is being influenced by fear, greed, panic, or a genuine need. This pause can prevent many impulsive mistakes.

Second, develop a mindset of financial discipline and self-control. Create a budget or a basic financial plan and make a conscious effort to follow it consistently, even when temptations arise.

Third, set clear financial goals for yourself. Once your goals are defined, prepare a realistic plan to achieve them and stick to it without getting distracted by short-term desires.

Fourth, avoid herd mentality. Do not spend or invest simply because others around you are doing so. What works for someone else may not suit your financial situation.

Finally, review your financial decisions regularly. This helps you understand which choices were driven by emotions and which were truly need-based. Improving your financial knowledge also clears confusion, builds confidence, and helps you make better and fewer mistakes in the future.

Developing healthy financial habits means following simple and practical practices over the long term. These habits help reduce financial stress, improve money management, and guide you toward financial security and stability.

One of the most important habits is **saving regularly**. This means setting aside a fixed amount from your monthly salary every month. Follow the principle of saving first and spending later and try to increase your savings gradually as your income grows.

Another key habit is **spending within your limits**. Be aware of how much you can comfortably spend and make sure your expenses stay within that range.

Creating a budget is also essential. Prepare a clear financial budget, review it regularly, and follow it with discipline to stay in control of your finances.

When it comes to **debt**, try to avoid borrowing unless it is truly necessary. Excessive loans can create stress, increase financial pressure, and negatively affect your credit score.

It is also important to **invest consistently**. Regular investing allows you to benefit from the power of compounding over time.

Finally, **review your finances periodically**, such as every quarter or every six months. This helps you identify areas where you can reduce expenses or increase savings. Above all, try to avoid emotional spending and make thoughtful, planned financial decisions.

Chapter 10: The Future of Personal Finance

Technological Innovations

Trends in Personal Finance

Adapting to Change

Continuous Learning and Improvement

Think of technology in finance as a helpful assistant that makes managing money easier, smarter, and more organized. If I were a normal person using today's tools, I would see financial technology as a way to simplify daily money decisions and prepare better for the future. Let's break this down in simple, human terms.

Technology has changed finance from something complex and time-consuming into something simple and accessible. Earlier, people depended on bank visits, paperwork, and manual tracking. Today, most financial activities can be done through a mobile phone.

Digital banking and payment systems allow individuals to transfer money, pay bills, check balances, and track transactions instantly. This improves control over money and reduces delays.

Budgeting and expense-tracking apps automatically record where money is spent. Instead of guessing, people can clearly see spending patterns and identify unnecessary expenses.

Online investment platforms and robotic advisors have made investing easier for everyone. These tools suggest investments based on goals, income, and risk tolerance, making professional-style guidance available to ordinary individuals.

AI-based financial tools analyze behavior, predict expenses, and give alerts, helping people avoid overspending and make better decisions.

As nothing is constant in the world so as the trends in financial world, Personal finance is moving towards more **automation, personalization, and intelligence**.

AI-driven personal finance assistants will act like digital financial coaches. They will guide budgeting, saving, and investing in real time, based on individual behavior.

Automation of savings and investments will increase. Money will automatically move into savings, emergency funds, or investments without the need for manual effort.

Cashless and paperless finance will become more common. Digital records, e-KYC, and online documentation will reduce paperwork and improve transparency.

Integrated financial platforms will combine banking, investing, insurance, and credit in one place, giving a complete financial picture.

With all these technological innovations and continuous chaining trends one must adapt these changes. Adapting to financial technology does not require expert knowledge—only openness and discipline.

First, individuals should **start small** by using basic tools like mobile banking and budgeting apps. Comfort grows with usage.

Second, improving **financial and digital awareness** is important. Understanding how tools work helps people trust and use them wisely.

Third, automation should be used carefully. While automated savings and investments are helpful, individuals must still review their finances regularly.

Fourth, **data security and privacy** should be taken seriously. Using trusted platforms, strong passwords, and two-factor authentication is essential.

Finally, technology should support—not replace—human judgment. Clear financial goals and disciplined habits remain the foundation of good financial health. Continuous learning on the technology and financial instruments is the need. In parallel when you work on your strategies and brainstorm, you will be able to improvise thema dn that can you your new learning.

Happy Financing.

www.ingramcontent.com/pod-product-compliance
Lightning Source LLC
LaVergne TN
LVHW052110210926
848482LV00024B/526

* 9 7 9 8 9 0 4 3 1 4 1 6 3 *